THE
GOOD NEWS CHAIR

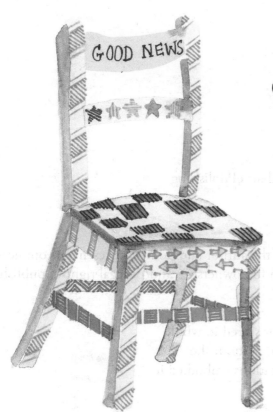

A simple tool for shaping a child's positive behavior and self-image

HARRIET ARKLEY

The Good News Chair: A Simple Tool for Shaping a Child's Positive Behavior and Self-Image.
Harriet Arkley
Print Version; Copyright ©2014 Harriet Arkley; All rights reserved.
eBook; Copyright ©2014 Harriet Arkley
Cover Design by Tony Locke, Armchair ePublishing
Cover Illustration by Marianne Dougan

Published by Harriet Arkley & Armchair ePublishing
ISBN: 978-0-615-98226-7
Library of Congress: 2014904565

Book layout and eBook, .epub, .pdf and .mobi conversions by Armchair ePublishing
www.armchair-epublishing.weebly.com
Anacortes, WA 98221

To learn more about the author or to order print copies, visit:
www.goodnewschair.com

Painting by Julie Alpert

Acknowledgements

Cyndi Spears, our beloved secretary at both Withrow and the Charter School, welcomed all good news as a diversion from the phone, piles of paperwork, and the constant stream of people who had business to do in the school office. In my absence, it was Cyndi who recorded the good news and saw that it went into the Charter School's newsletter.

A special note of thanks to Rebecca Davis, a student at the Ball Charter School. As a 4th grader Rebecca offered to help illustrate this book. Rebecca is now grown up and a journalism major at Illinois State University.

Thankfully, I found Cami Ostman early on. As my enthusiastic and skillful writing coach, she guided me as I wrote this story. Kari Neumeyer, as my copy editor, helped with the flow of the story. Amanda Hagarty stepped in as I joined Facebook and created my webpage www.goodnewschair.com. Alice Acheson took yet another hard look and suggested a new direction.

Naida Grunden, Andi Elliott, Jan Sullivan, Donna Neal, and Lindsay Neal all read the manuscript through the eyes of parents and teachers. Their cheerleading was invaluable.

Susan Hirst and Kathy Barrett took Chairs into their homes and used them with grandchildren. Jennifer Pittis and Kelly Glynn, both primary elementary teachers, put Chairs in their classrooms and helped to think about how Chairs might be used in classrooms.

Marianne Dougan did the happy design for the current version of the Chair. Diane Tate opened her basement work area, making it possible for my husband and me to paint five more Chairs. Doug Bascom gets all the credit for photographing the Chair. Julie Alpert painted my cherished logo.

Thanks especially to Andy, Todd, and Jed, our sons, who to this day have a lot of good news to share with our family and their friends. Finally a standing ovation to my husband, Alfred, who for 48 years has supported and promoted my work with young children.

Painting by Julie Alpert

TABLE OF CONTENTS

Foreword

"THINK LEFT AND THINK RIGHT AND THINK LOW AND THINK HIGH.
OH, THE THINKS YOU CAN THINK UP IF ONLY YOU TRY!"
— Dr. Seuss: *OH THE THINKS YOU CAN THINK!* (1971)

Dear Teachers and Parents,

This book is for those of you who are attracted to the principles and practices of positive reinforcement or the power of using a carrot rather than a stick. This is the story of one way two schools did just that. The Good News Chair was the centerpiece of this effort. The Chair sat in my office as the principal of two schools, but it works just as well in a classroom or a home.

As teachers, you see how a Good News Chair can support a classroom and/or school management plan, alter the classroom culture, or be tied to the academic program. Could it be a place to share:
- helping a classmate?
- following a classroom rule?
- completing an assignment in a timely manner?
- moving to a new reading level?
- getting to school on time?

Parents take note. Recognizing and celebrating accomplishments will lead to more of the same. Many behaviors and events qualify. A demonstration of responsible or moral behavior, an act of kindness, an athletic or academic feat are just a few examples of what can be shared in the Chair. What might a Good News Chair do for your family? Could it be a place to share:
- an improvement on a report card?
- the end of thumb sucking?

- a good play on the soccer field?
- a family trip?
- trying broccoli for the first time?
- the promotion at work?
- getting along with a sibling?
- a clean room?

The Chair is a simple tool to help your child(ren), grandchildren or students go forth in the world feeling confident, worthy, special, and secure. I will tell you about the birth of the Good News Chair, how it worked in two schools, classrooms, and homes, what was shared in the Chair, and how to make and use of your very own Chair. There will be space in the book too, to record your very own good news.

My best to all of you and your children,

Harriet Arkley

I feel happy
because you're always
there when I go to the
Good News
chair

Peter

Chapter 1

The Birth of the Good News Chair

"ALL DOORS ARE HARD TO UNLOCK UNTIL YOU HAVE THE KEY."
—Robert C. O'Brien: *MRS. FRISBY AND THE RATS OF NIMH* (1971)

I was an elementary school principal for eleven years. After a number of years as a school teacher, followed by a decade devoted to raising three sons, I was eager for the challenge. I began by enrolling in a doctoral program in curriculum and instruction. This was followed by a position as an administrator for the Springfield Public Schools in Springfield, Illinois. Fortunately, I was in the school district's central office when the state earmarked funds to serve at-risk three-to-five-year-olds and their families. In addition, there were funds available to create a parent education program for parents of children from birth through the age of three. With these funds, we created citywide programs open to young children and their parents. With these experiences as a backdrop, I was ready to try my hand as a school principal.

My first assignment as principal was at Withrow, a Springfield public early childhood school designed to meet the needs of nearly 500 three-to-five-year-olds. These children were enrolled in this school because of some unmet need. Poverty, crime, drugs, birth defects, mental illness, language delays, and chronic illnesses all found their way through the front door. We were determined to make a difference in the lives of these young children and their families. Supported by a substantial body of research, we knew that "beginning at the beginning" would pay off for the children, their parents, and our society. The National Association for the Education of Young Children (NAEYC) keeps track of studies regarding the long-term effects of an early intervention. A higher rate of high school graduation, a lower arrest rate, and lower rates of grade retention are just some of the key findings.

1

I knew ahead of time that the part of the job I would not like much was the time spent handling discipline. Most can recount some fearful memory around being "sent to the office."

I wanted as little of that kind of energy in my school as possible. It is a fact, however, that behaviors such as talking back, stealing, bullying, kicking, swearing, and peeing contests in the boys' bathroom often land children in "the office." In my school, like most other elementary schools, there was not an assistant in charge of discipline. There was not even a school nurse to mop up the bloody noses, bandage the skinned knees, or on some days to check for lice. That left a secretary (exceptionally able but overworked), the custodian (off mopping up yet another mess) and the cook (who had better be getting lunch ready). And me.

Almost by accident, I figured out how to save hours every week from handling misbehavior. At the same time I like to think I found a way to personally encourage learning, effort, accomplishments, and school manners, all things the teachers were doing every minute of the day in their classrooms. And since Early Childhood educators are a hopeful, dedicated, and often playful bunch, I knew they were primed for what was about to happen.

Barney, an enormous purple dinosaur figure, had caught the attention of the children in the school. Barney was everywhere in 1991. He was on TV, DVDs, T-shirts, balloons, lunch boxes, and sold, too, in the form of a stuffed toy. In one of Barney's best known songs, he sings, "I love you, you love me, we're a great big family with a great big hug and a kiss from me to you, won't you say you me love too?" In spite of the critics who found his message too simple and sweet, the teachers and I found his message and his buoyant personality just what our kids needed.

Barney became our school mascot. With PTA funds, we bought a four-foot stuffed Barney. He showed up in school pictures, on opening day, at assemblies, and at all other important occasions, becoming our ever-present symbol of positivity. After a birthday party we had for Barney, a boy told his teacher, "I believe in the Easter Bunny, Santa Claus, Barney, Baby Bop and God."

In the middle of our love affair with Barney, a parent found a small purple wooden chair in the shape of our beloved mascot. For the next seven years the Barney Chair sat in my office in a prominent spot seen by everyone who came into the school office. Children naturally wanted to sit in the Barney Chair. Over time this was allowed and encouraged when a child had "good news" to share. The good news children brought to the Chair covered a wide range of topics; a step taken without the aid of a crutch, a potty training victory, the mastery of the alphabet, a loose tooth, a new sister or brother, or an appropriate substitution for a temper tantrum. All were reasons for a visit to the Barney Chair.

Without really meaning to, we had stumbled onto something really special and effective in terms of changing the meaning of coming to (or being sent to) "the office." I began to see how Barney's Good News Chair might encourage the learning and behavior we were teaching.

Lynn was three when she came to Withrow. Born with cerebral palsy, she came through the front door on the first day pushing a little pink plastic shopping cart. The cart kept her upright and moving forward but we knew she had to learn to walk on her own. After months of help from Lynn's teacher, the physical therapist, and her parents, she began to step out on her own. What a day that was! Soon after her first solo steps, Lynn's teacher brought her to the office to sit in the Barney Chair. In her own words Lynn announced to us what she had done. The little pink plastic shopping cart was nowhere to be seen. There wasn't a dry eye in the place.

Routinely, other children popped into the office to announce that they could write their own name, or that they were no longer biting when they got mad, or that they were at school on time. These were three-to-five-year-olds so a teacher or a parent usually accompanied them. We all cheered at their reports. Slowly but surely a few minutes in the Barney Chair became a new way to acknowledge and celebrate progress. I began to see how the Chair could support a school culture that focused on the learning, citizenship, and self-confidence that we were promoting rather than on the children's deficits or handicaps.

Over time we all noticed that the "good news" visits were outnumbering the "bad news" visits to the office. Wrapped around all of this was a faculty who always looked for ways to encourage desirable behavior by celebrating all victories, from the tiny to truly life-changing. With these capable and positive teachers and staff, we created a place where children would have a better chance of growing up as happy and healthy kids. The Good News Chair was a permanent and important part of our school community. The Chair was our own brand of positive reinforcement.

But was the practice of having a special Chair in my office transferable or was the Barney Chair just a happy fluke that worked for the young children at Withrow? I was about to find out.

In 1998 I left Withrow School when I was chosen to be the first principal of a new charter school in Springfield, Illinois. The Springfield Ball Charter School was an outgrowth of a partnership between the school district and Carl Ball, a businessman with a foundation and an ambitious vision for schools. This school was designed to ultimately serve preschoolers through eighth-graders. I had to leave Barney and his Good News Chair behind. But what would take its place in my new office?

The summer before the Charter School opened I spotted an old oak school chair left behind in a district

BALL CHARTER'S CHAIR

warehouse and I knew just what to do. I painted it with brightly colored stripes, stars, and polka dots and placed it in my office to become Springfield Ball Charter's very own Good News Chair. I invited the new students to stop by and share their good news.

The youngest and the oldest in our new school found their way to the Good News Chair just as the children back at Withrow had. The act of stating their news in their very own words ended up being very self-validating. Teachers and parents reported that children repeated and built on the "good news" both in the classroom and at home. In the classroom, this could mean that a child advanced in reading or more consistently followed the classroom rules. At home, this could mean that the child chose to "play school" or was more helpful with siblings.

This led us to begin using the Good News Chair more intentionally. Charlie is a terrific example of this. Charlie's mother drove him to and from school. Because the office was right inside the front door, we noticed that Charlie was late to school most mornings. He would come into the office, sheepishly report his tardiness, and scoot down to class. His teacher reported that Charlie was missing the announcements and instructions she gave to start the day. Charlie reported that his mother was always "running late." His mother reported that Charlie was "slow as molasses" in the morning. Could morning visits to the Good News Chair help change this pattern? I explained to both Charlie and his mom how Charlie's tardiness was affecting his school day and suggested that if they arrived on time they might both stop by for a short visit on the Chair. It worked! The next morning Charlie and his mom showed up, came in the office and reported that they had "run early and fast." In the future they rarely were tardy and Charlie's school days got off to a good start.

Sometimes, too, the Chair gave us insight into what a child was learning. Edward, a kindergartner, after hearing a story about Martin Luther King Jr. not being able to play with a white child, said, "A person is a person. A color is a color." This was good news.

Unlike my former school, the Charter School attracted children from throughout the community, those who swam at country clubs and those who swam at the aging city pool studied together. News from everyone was recorded in journals and published monthly in the school newsletter. The Good News column turned out to be a hit, often the first thing parents and their children read. In this way, the Good News Chair brought the community together.

The small purple Barney Chair started this all. The first child who plopped down in that chair and announced that he had something he wanted to tell me gave me an idea about a new way I could encourage all aspects of learning and positive self-image. I believe that my discovery is transferable to any school, home, camp, or club where children and adults interact with one another.

You will see in the entries that follow what "Good News" looked like on a daily basis and how this chair celebrated all that we valued: Learning, accomplishments, effort, the connection between family and school, and finally, a child's world. The Good News Chair can do the same for the children in your life.

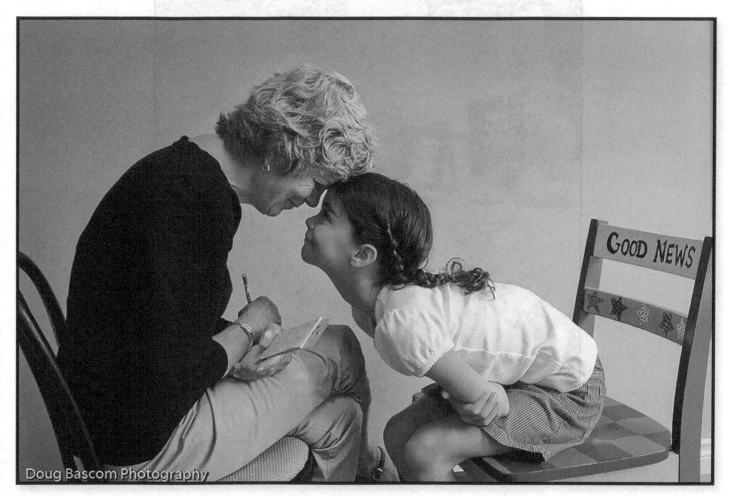

THE AUTHOR AND HER GRANDDAUGHTER

WE WON!

Chapter 2

How did the Good News Chair Work in the Schools?

"I ASSURE YOU THAT YOU CAN PICK UP MORE INFORMATION WHEN YOU ARE LISTENING
THAN WHEN YOU ARE TALKING."
—E.B. White: *THE TRUMPET OF THE SWAN* (1970)

Visits to the Chair were handled differently at Withrow Early Childhood Center and at Springfield Ball Charter School. Withrow served three-to-five-year-olds while Ball Charter's doors were open to three-to-ten-year-olds. Faculty at Withrow never let the little ones out of their sight while the older children at Springfield Ball Charter were often permitted to walk on their own from one part of the building to another. At both Withrow and Ball Charter I recorded the good news in journals.

At Withrow, the classroom teacher or her aide usually prompted visits to the Good News Chair. Since it was clear that many of the children were from homes where rules and standards for behavior were both casual and inconsistent, we knew that the first order of business was to help them learn the rules that would make their classrooms and the school run smoothly. This took some time, more so with the few that had an especially hard time following directions. So visits to the Chair were often to acknowledge that a child had followed a particular rule. Coming when called after recess, putting away supplies or treating a classmate kindly were all good reasons for a celebratory trip to the office.

Now and then, a visit to the Chair was followed by a good laugh. This happened once right before Christmas. One of Withrow's preschool teachers was leading her class to the library. Jerry, age four, noticed the red fire alarm mounted on the hallway wall. He stopped, studied it for some time, and announced to his class that he knew exactly what it was. With conviction, he told his teacher that it was Santa's camera. His classmates nodded in agreement and off they went to the library. Jerry's teacher knew this was a "good one," one I would want to put in my Good News journal. When she had a minute, she brought Jerry to the office. We all gathered around to listen. When they left we doubled up in laughter and ended up telling the story over and over again. Jerry's teacher claimed that her class straightened up and quieted down every time they passed by "Santa's camera."

SANTA'S CAMERA

At Ball Charter the children were older, but I was still determined that the Chair would occupy an important place in my office. It would be one way for the school to celebrate learning, good citizenship and much more. I took the Chair to one of the first faculty meetings and explained how it would work. I urged teachers to send children to the Chair when there was something noteworthy to celebrate. Nearly all of the Good News journal entries were printed in the school newspaper.

Now and then, a teacher sat in the Chair herself and shared some good news. On the first day of school, a kindergarten teacher came in to share a story. Her students walked to school from a neighborhood with high poverty and crime rates. Most of these children had not been inside a school, but at the same time, their parents had done the best they could to prepare them. To gauge what they knew about school, she asked her class, "What do you know about school?" The first child to respond was Evan who said, "We do our ABCs. We Color. We do everything God wants us to do." And with that the year began. It was a good sign but there was still a lot of work to be done.

At other times, I noticed something a child did and brought them to the Chair myself. One day, for example, I was supervising the playground and noticed three third-graders picking up litter. I invited them into my office and then recorded the story and put in the school newsletter. There was rarely another piece of trash on the playground after that.

Now and then, a child just stopped by and asked for a turn on the Chair. This often happened as school opened or was getting ready to close. Because a number of children were dropped off or picked up by parents, they ended up passing by the office. We all stifled a laugh when a three-year-old came in and announced that, "I can poo in the toilet." You see this was an entrance requirement for our preschool program at Ball Charter and the pressure was on at home to get toilet training done.

Parents used the Good News Chair too. After a recital, a game, a family trip or the birth of a baby, they would prompt a child to drop in for a visit. (We suspected that they liked seeing their news in the school newsletter.)

Did I ever see the visits to the Chair as an interruption to my busy days? No, not really. If my door was closed, children knew they needed to come back later. Or my secretary, a master of balancing dozens of tasks at one time, often dropped everything to record some news. The Chair, as the key part of a positive reward system, was easy for others to use.

The fact was that these visits brightened a day in the office for all of us who worked there. As you would guess, a lot of the work in the office had to do with solving problems, handling personnel issues, setting and implementing new policies and curriculum, talking with angry or upset parents, or monitoring a budget. Listening to good news from the children we served dropped sunshine into often difficult days. After all, the focus at Withrow was to get young children off to a strong start and the motto of Springfield Ball Charter was, "A Place Where Children Are The Priority." Acknowledging Good News was one way I could keep track of how we were doing.

Parents and grandparents will see in Chapter 4 how the Good News Chair works in a home. The use of positive reinforcement is just as important at home as it is inside the schoolhouse doors. Many child development experts have argued that an encouraging and positive atmosphere at home is the greatest gift a parent can give a child.

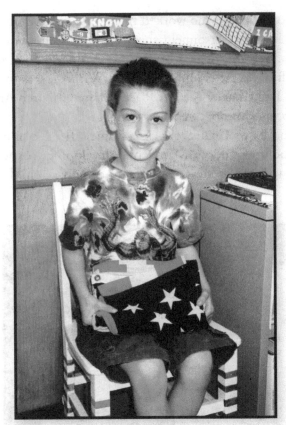

FLAG DAY

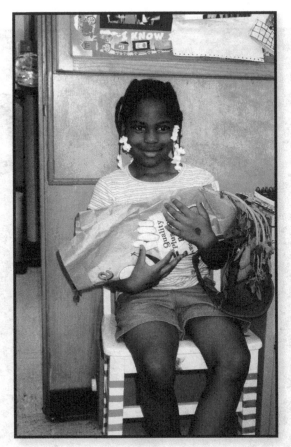

VEGETABLES FROM THE SCHOOL
GARDEN

Chapter 3

Views from the Chair

"EACH THING SHE LEARNED BECAME PART OF HERSELF, TO BE USED OVER AND OVER IN NEW ADVENTURES."
—Kate Seredy: *GYPSY* (1951)

You have read about the "birth" of the Chair and a few stories about what happened when children sat down. You know how children came to have a turn in the Chair. Now for the best part. Here you will read about some of what the children shared and what I recorded in journals. You will begin to imagine what your child(ren) or students might want to share, both at school and at home.

I rarely knew ahead of time what news was coming through the door. Children themselves determined the topics. News of good behavior, discoveries, learning, pets, siblings and families, lost or loose teeth, accomplishments, milestones, and sometimes heartfelt confessions all found their way to the Chair.

Some have asked whether there was a Bad News Chair. No, not really. A standard issue plastic office chair did just fine for time outs and hard talks.

Good Behavior

"I DON'T MIND HIM THINKING," SAID MRS. BROWN, WITH A WORRIED EXPRESSION ON
HER FACE. "IT'S WHEN HE ACTUALLY THINKS OF SOMETHING THAT THE TROUBLE STARTS."
—Michael Bond: *A BEAR CALLED PADDINGTON* (1958)

Even though they often came to tell me good news, children were still sent to the office for misbehaving, too.
Time-outs, calls to parents, the loss of privileges, counseling, and heart-to-hearts were still often the business of
the principal. At the same time, a spell in the Good News Chair was an acknowledgement of both small and big
personal victories. In their own words, children had to identify exactly what it was that they had done to earn a few
minutes in the Chair.

Robin, quite tall and muscular for his age, was a second-grader who came from a rough neighborhood and
family where fist-fights happened daily. While we could not change the neighborhood or his family, we made it
clear that arguments could not be settled at school by physical means. This was a tough lesson to learn and took lots
and lots of practice and coaching. Imagine, then, the day that Robin sat in the Good News Chair and announced,
"A kid spit on me. I calmed myself down and told the teacher instead of spitting back." Was this the end of Robin's
troubles? Oh no, but it was the beginning of a change.

Some more good behavior news:
• Nate has been insulting me by calling me names, etc. I have been able to ignore him.
Cameron, age 9

• I followed the rules for two whole days. It was kind of hard and kind of easy.
MacKinze, age 7

Easy and consistent was what we were looking for! These were little victories but there were more to come.

• I haven't cried once today.
Sean, age 5

• I am so proud. Tomorrow will be the same.
Sean, age 6 (one year later)

For Sean the slightest frustration brought tears. His was a long and hard road to recovery. With the help of a counselor, his parents, and a caring teacher, his sense of self-worth and self-control grew.

• I am learning how to be a leader.
Kiana, age 8

Kiana was a leader but sometimes led her classmates astray. We were determined to help her use her popularity in more constructive ways. With guidance in the classroom and on the playground Kiana learned more about sharing, cooperating, and setting an example for younger students.

• I learned about sharing and helping other people. And telling them how to do their work so they won't mess up.
Kendall, age 5

• I helped Rebecca when she got hurt.
Kailey, age 6

Acknowledging compassion always seemed like a perfect reason for a trip to the Good News Chair.

I AM LEARNING HOW TO BE ON A TEAM. DAVID, AGE 8

Discoveries about the Big Wide Wonderful World

"SO MANY THINGS ARE POSSIBLE JUST AS LONG AS YOU DON'T KNOW THEY'RE IMPOSSIBLE."
—Norton Juster: *THE PHANTOM TOLLBOOTH* (1961)

Children thrive on learning new things about their world. It is the reason they ask so many questions and want to report on just about everything under the sun. Our school encouraged inquiry and celebrated it in all of its forms.

Discoveries came in all shapes and forms:

• In Miss Baxter's class our worms are pregnant and are having babies. We have seen two egg sacs and three babies.
  Felicia, age 9 and Ronicia, age 9

• I found a fossil (trileabite) when digging in my backyard. I'm going to be a scientist when I grow up.
  Eric, age 8

The natural world was a big draw. The playground was edged by a forest and each class had its own garden plot. Discoveries happened on a daily basis in both places but were most often shared right back in the classroom.

• Our bus monitor is the first black female in the world to fly an F16. She is also a boxer and fake boxed with Muhammad Ali's daughter.
  Ryan, age 9, Jayme, age 10, Swayce, age 8

Hmmmm? I wondered…

• I discovered that James Howe has a very good sense of humor, especially in his book The Celery Stalks at Midnight.
  Walker, age 8

Oh yes, we loved news about children learning to read and write.

Learning the ABCs

"FATE HAS DECREED THAT ALL LAZY BOYS WHO COME TO HATE BOOKS AND SCHOOLS AND TEACHERS AND SPEND ALL THEIR DAYS WITH BOYS AND GAMES MAY SOONER OR LATER TURN INTO DONKEYS."
—C. Colodi: *THE ADVENTURES OF PINOCCHIO* (1883)

The White House, state capitals, schools, our communities, and all parents expect children to learn in school. What, how much, and exactly how are often disputed but all can agree that literacy and numeracy should be served as the main course. The Good News Chair was a place where we celebrated learning in all of its manifestations. In the end, it was our ultimate goal.

Literacy, or learning to read and write, was a core value in both Withrow and the Charter school. Teachers devoted most of their day to these lessons. Books were everywhere. We posted examples of writing on both classroom and hallway walls for children and visitors to read. Imagine one teacher's delight when I told her that seven-year-old Morgan plopped down in the Chair and announced that she had discovered something, "In my journal I wrote, 'I don't need to make a wish because I am happy just the way I am. All I need is a book to go where I want to go'." Wow.

Amelia, a tiny and sad little girl, had just started kindergarten when she walked into my office and asked for a turn on the Good News Chair. I had noticed that her talented teacher was giving her students an opportunity to write each day. I also had noted that these kindergarten students were learning how to use what they knew about letter sounds as they tried to spell words. So I was convinced that Amelia was catching on when she showed me her journal entry. It read, "ILIKETOGOSOWPOL." I knew that was in fact, "I like to go to the swimming pool."

Math

• We figured out how many trees Johnny Appleseed planted. The answer is 151,680,000.
Brian, age 9 and Daniel, age 8

A little known fact?

• I figured out 46 ways to write the number 24.
Tim, age 9

• Me and my mom were talking. I want to start a math club. My mom said to present the idea to you.
Jacob, age 8

We did just that thanks to a parent who offered to lead the club.

• I counted our money from our garage sale. It was $504. I can also do fractions.
John, age 6 ½

Writing

• I have never wrote a whole page but today I wrote a whole page about my dad.
 Samantha, age 5

• I edited my writing today and added capitals and periods.
 Dylan, age 7

Language

• We can sing Twinkle, Twinkle, Little Star in Spanish.
Holly, age 5, Micalister, age 5, Joy, age 5

• I have been enjoying this school because it helps you get smart and teaches you Spanish.
Jasmine, age 9

• I can make the sound of the letter w.
Crystal, age 5

A huge accomplishment and all thanks to our talented speech therapist.

Pets

"I WISH WE HAD TAILS TO WAG," SAID MR. DEARLY
—Dodie Smith: *101 DALMATIONS* (1957)

News about pets made it to the Good News Chair, too. Here are a few entries. Our favorites came from Matthew. His always shared these reports with a good deal of drama and more details than we could ever record.

• I got a lizard. Her name is Jenny. She hates frozen crickets. She likes meal worms.
Matthew, age 7

• My lizard stopped hibernating. I was afraid she was dead.
Matthew, age 7

• I got the family's dog. His name is Fritz. I was the only one who took care of him and let him sleep on my bed.
Matthew, age 8

• We lost our dog. After seven hours we found him in our van. He had been asleep the whole time.
Matthew, age 9

FOR MY BIRTHDAY I GOT A TOY STUFFED DOG. I WAS HOPING FOR A REAL DOG.
ANNA, AGE 6

Siblings and Family

"WHERE YOU LOVE SOMEBODY A WHOLE LOT, AND YOU KNOW THAT PERSON LOVES YOU, THAT'S THE MOST BEAUTIFUL PLACE IN THE WORLD."
—Ann Cameron: *THE MOST BEAUTIFUL PLACE IN THE WORLD* (1988)

The parents of our students were often young and consumed with new babies and raising their families. Those of us in the office loved celebrating this part of a child's life. It reminded us over and over again how the children's lives at home influenced their school days.

At six years old, red-haired Alexandria was the oldest in a family that seemed every couple of years to grow in size. She kept us up to date on these pregnancies and the newest baby in their home. One day she could not wait to tell me that, "Last night I saw the baby move in Mom's stomach." Joy was wrapped around these announcements. At the same time they served as a reminder that this oldest and most responsible little girl might welcome a little extra attention from time to time.

New Babies:

• I'm a new big brother. In celebration, my Dad is going to have lunch with me!
Ryan, age 7

• My mom is getting wired up to have a baby today. Her name will be Mackenzie.
Morgan, age 8

• Mom will be home with my new baby sister. They'll be there when I get home.
Morgan, age 8

• My aunt had a new baby girl. We're going to Indiana to see her. They fixed the holes in her heart.
Sela, age 7

• I just got a new baby sister. She's not out yet though.
Erin, age 5

More news from the home front:

• I met my brother for the first time yesterday. He's 24.
Ronicia, age 7 ½

• Cressa is getting a new big bed, no more crib.
Madeline, age 4

• I have great news. My Dad is going out of town.
Latashia, age 6

• I'm going to my brother's graduation in May. He's
getting the highest certificate (sum cum laude) he can get.
We're having a big party.
   Sean, age 7

• My grandma is coming today. I like to help her bake
cookies and play games.
   Raya, age 5

• My grandma is here from Canada and Australia. She makes great chicken soup.
Chloe, age 6 and Norma (Grandma), age 67

• My mom is getting married again. He's great.
Brooke, age 9

Accomplishments

"I THINK I CAN. I THINK I CAN. I THINK I CAN."
—Watty Piper: *THE LITTLE ENGINE THAT COULD* (1930)

From a new haircut to a successful recital to learning to whistle, we heard it all. I never knew for sure what was coming through the door. These were generally spontaneous and personal. They were often delivered as children came into the school in the morning.

Now and then I learned something about what was happening in a classroom. Instead of celebrating the Christmas holiday at Ball Charter, we put on what we called "A Trip Around the World." Each class worked on a presentation about a particular country and subsequently we all took turns visiting each classroom. In some rooms these projects were very ambitious and frankly a sore spot with the custodian who often mopped up the mess. One year Mrs. Baxter, a new upper-grade teacher, allowed her students to turn the classroom into a jungle. Oh my. So it should not have come as a surprise when Jackie, age 9, sat in the Good News Chair and reported that, "My teacher chose only five people to paint the mural and she didn't kill us when we got paint on the floor."

The children shared all manner of accomplishments with such pride:

• I'm six. I'm learning the alphabet and how to do it. I'm learning how to act like a big kid and to be good.
Thomas, age 6

• I can tie my own shoes. I can even put my socks on.
Elle, age 4

• I got through my dance recital. I didn't have to watch the teacher that much.
Elaina, age 6

• I cut my hair one foot. I gave it to Locks of Love
Jenny, age 10

• Today I'm going to a baking show with my dad. He won third place with his zucchini bread.
Samantha, age 6

• I read three straight hours last night. My dad said I couldn't watch television.
Monica, age 9

• I had stage fright about talking in front of my class but I practiced a couple of times by myself and I was fine.
Rebecca, age 7

• I can whistle like a big boy.
Beck, age 3

• Between the time we left and we arrived we missed the tornado.
John, age 38 (Parent)

Yes, even parents and teachers sometimes came in for a turn in the Good News Chair. This was a close call at the end of the school day. John, a father of one of our students, had left work to pick up his son at school and narrowly missed being hit by a tornado.

• I don't pee in my bed anymore.
Joy, age 4

• I'm almost not afraid of Turner. I'm going step by step. The step now is that I'm not afraid of him when he's on the leash.
Madison, age 5 ½

Madison was terrified of all dogs. Turner was my golden retriever who came to school now and then. After a few years Madison took Turner for a walk and in turn I held her pet snake, a first for me.

• I've decided to donate $1 each month to the school. This will go until I'm old and gray.
Danielle, age 8

• I am the new Worm Princess.
Tye, age 6

To be the Worm Princess in this classroom you had to know five facts about worms. Her teacher had a composting worm bin in the classroom.

• Yesterday I helped a sub bus driver get to the next stop.
Colin, age 10

Colin regularly got pink slips from the bus driver for breaking the bus rules.

Teeth

"EVERY TIME A CHILD SAYS, "I DON'T BELIEVE IN FAIRIES," THERE IS A FAIRY SOMEWHERE THAT FALLS DOWN DEAD."
— J.M. Barrie: *PETER PAN* (1911)

Suffice it to say that I helped celebrate hundreds of lost teeth. The first loss is a big day, no doubt about it. As adults we lose teeth in accidents, in the chairs of oral surgeons, and from old age. None are happy events. In the life of a child, however, a loose or lost tooth is a thing of wonder, a milestone, something that results in a magical visit by the tooth fairy.

• I FINALLY lost a tooth. The Tooth Fairy left a note and tied it with red ribbon.
Jesse, age 7 ½

• I lost my tooth yesterday morning. The tooth fairy didn't come. Mom said it was too windy.
 Ben, age 7

• I lost my third tooth but the Tooth Fairy left my tooth. I wonder why?
Noah, age 6

• I lost my front teeth. My mom says I talk like an old man.
Adrian, age 7

• I lost a big back tooth. It's been bugging me for months.
Jacob, age 10

• I lost a tooth when my brother punched me in the mouth. It wasn't even loose!
 Savannah, age 7

• I'm going to be losing one of my dog teeth in a few weeks. My dad says it's worth $15 bucks.
 Tyler, age 8

Firsts or Milestones

"YOU'VE GOT TO MAKE THOSE DARING LEAPS OR YOU'RE NOWHERE," SAID MUSKRAT.
—Russell Hoban: *THE MOUSE AND THE CHILD* (1967)

Years before a first date, a driver's license, or turning 21, there are many others "firsts" that are important milestones. My guess is that the milestones reported in the Good News Chair are remembered today.

Ryan was being raised by a loving grandmother but desperately wanted a big brother, a father, an uncle, or an adult male friend to spend time with. He could hardly wait to get to the Good News Chair to share his news. He had just met Rocky, a young adult who came from the Big Brothers Big Sisters program. Ryan was seven when he met Rocky and shared, "I got my Big Brother! We went sledding, played my Battleship game, and looked at pictures, and scooped snow." A few years later he shared, "Tomorrow Rocky and I are going to the Big Brother banquet and getting an award as a great match."

The standard entries in the Good News Journal weren't all as significant as Ryan's but some were definitely noteworthy:

• I went to Texas and saw the ocean for the first time
Chantil, age 11

Me and Shelby tried eating alligator. We'll never do it again
Sela, age 7

• Last night there was a bat in my house. We all screamed. My brother's cat injured it. My Dad finished it off.
Laura, age 8

• I dreamed about a dragon. I fighted it and ate it all.
Alexis, age 4

Confessions

"THE TIME HAS COME," THE WALRUS SAID,
"TO TALK OF MANY THINGS:
OF SHOES – AND SHIPS – AND SEALING WAX –
OF CABBAGES AND KINGS."
—Lewis Carroll: *THROUGH THE LOOKING CLASS* (1872)

What we called confessions weren't the kind that you might make in church. They were, however, apt to take your breath away or put a smile on everyone's face. We liked to have the day end with what we called a "confession." You will see why.

• When I was a baby I didn't let anyone take the pacifier out of my mouth.
Kendall, age 5

• My sister, Rachel, came to school. Unfortunately, the class guinea pig peed on her.
Matthew, age 6

• I went to The King and I. I loved it but I fell asleep in the middle.
Callista, age 5

• I brought Sara, my doll, to school. She's named after my aunt. She is naked. She is in big trouble.
Madeline, age 4

• I went to the fair and got lost. The police took me home.
Karran, age 8

• I found out I didn't have an ear infection, just a little bug (she was thinking an insect) in my ear.
Rebecca, age 6

• I saved myself from being hit by a delivery car.
Molly, age 10

• I finally got the nerve to wear a dress.
Jamie, age 12

• I'm glad I go to this school. I love it.
Rebecca, age 4

So, as you can see, there are many uses for the Good News Chair, but the most important thing is that it gives children a chance to tell about their experiences in their own words.

BROTHERS AND BEST BUDDIES

HERE'S HOW YOU DO IT...

Chapter 4

Getting Started with Your Own Good News Chair

"I WANT TO SAY THAT WONDERFUL IDEAS CAN COME FROM ANYWHERE. SOMETIMES YOU MAKE A MISTAKE, BREAK SOMETHING, OR LOSE A HAT, AND THE NEXT THING YOU KNOW, YOU GET A GREAT IDEA."
—Maira Kalman: *MAX MAKES A MILLION* (1990)

Making Your Chair

The photographs in this book are intended to give you an idea of what your Good News Chair could look like. No two will be the same! You might end up using a stool, a bench, a tree stump or a saddle rather than a traditional chair. In fact, those I used in my school office look different from the ones I painted for this book. The important thing is to make the Chair a special place for your child.

I found old wooden chairs in used furniture stores, the back of school warehouses, in garages, and in stores dedicated to recycling. You can find them anywhere. To write "Good News" across the back, one of the slats needs to be wide and flat enough for the lettering.

1. The first order of business is to remove soil and excess old paint or varnish. "Rough up" the surface, as most old chairs have a coat of shellac or varnish that can prevent new paint from sticking. Both a small sander and a hand-held block sander are useful when taking a finish off. Use a lint-free cloth to wipe the chair clean once it has been completely sanded.

2. Apply a good primer coat that will act as a base for a water-based enamel or acrylic paint.

3. Children love primary colors. Use bold colors for your version of the chair. To get full coverage, brush on two coats of your favorite paint. Have fun deciding on a pattern and colors.

4. Be patient. The paint needs to "harden" for a few days.

Must one go to all of this work? Absolutely not! Remember, what really makes the Chair special is the experience the child will have from getting the full and positive attention from an adult.

Good News Chairs have now sat not only in a principal's office but also in classrooms and in the homes of parents and grandparents.

Tips From Classroom Teachers

All the teachers I spoke with agree that the teacher needs to introduce the Chair (with a little "Ta da!") and then talk to the children about how and when the Chair will be used. Here's what else they say:

• Let the children share whatever they feel is good news. News can range from sharing about a camping trip, to getting a new stuffed animal, to a geocaching adventure, to reading a chapter book for the first time, to finding a chrysalis, to visiting a father who is in jail. The child decides what is "good."

• In addition to letting students share whatever they want, the Chair can be used to recognize achievement of a particular classroom goal. Learning a set of number facts or spelling all words correctly on a spelling test might warrant a trip to the Good News Chair. Likewise, a student who shows kindness or respect can sit in the chair to share exactly what they (or another) student has done. Using the Chair this way will reinforce an academic and/or citizenship standard.

• Require students to sign up for a turn in the Chair. One teacher asked her students to write their good news down before they sat in the chair, giving them another reason to write during the day.

• Think of sharing as a way to give students an opportunity to speak in front of the class, listen to a classmate, and ask questions of one another; skills that need to be taught and practiced anyway.

• Capture the good news and send it home in the class newsletter as another way of sharing with parents what is going on at school. Dr. Haim Ginot wrote, "If you want your children to improve, let them overhear the nice things you say about them to others."

Tips from Parents and Grandparents

Parents and grandparents agree that their own enthusiasm for the Good News Chair is the determining factor as to how the Chair is used. Here is their advice:

• Put the chair in a prominent place where the family regularly gathers, thus reminding children of good news they may want to share. One family found that sharing their good news around the kitchen island worked just fine, no need for a special Chair.

• Give full attention to the child who is sitting in the chair.

• Encourage children to report the best part of their day if they can't think of their own good news.

• Set aside a special time for sharing in the family. Right after dinner works well. It can also be effective to leave the timing up to the child(ren).

• Write down the news as children report it. This way what is talked about becomes a written record of both big and little milestones in children's lives.

• Use the Good News Chair to offer insight on what is going well rather on negative behavior. Parent and grandparents agree that there are enough time-out chairs around to catch the stories of what has gone wrong.

The Good News Chair is a prop or reminder to catch children doing well. Parents, grandparents, and teachers can shape a child's positive behavior. Forest W. Witcraft said it well when he wrote, "A hundred years from now, it will not matter what your bank account was, the sort of house you lived in, or the kind of car you drove. But the world may be a little different because you were important in the life of someone young."

Good Eating

Taking Notes

Chapter 5

My Own Good News

"AS HUMAN BEINGS, OUR JOB IN LIFE IS TO HELP PEOPLE REALIZE HOW RARE
AND VALUABLE EACH ONE OF US REALLY IS..."
—Fred Rogers: *YOU ARE SPECIAL, NEIGHBORLY WIT AND WISDOM FROM MR. ROGERS, 2002*

Now it is your turn. Take a few minutes to listen to your child(ren) tell about something that is going well, something that they are proud of. Write it down and give it a date. This record could be better than a baby book. Watch what happens!

HARRIET ARKLEY

My Own Good News

My Own Good News

HARRIET ARKLEY

My Own Good News

My Own Good News

Keeping Track of the Good News

Memories of the Good News Chair

By the kids in Mrs. Robinson's First/Second Grade Class

Erin — I got to go to the Good News Chair when I read my first chapter book.

Lynn — I like the Good News Chair because it is special.

Kirby — I got to go to the Good News Chair when I wrote a whole page in my writer's notebook.

Justice — I like the Good News Chair because you are there!

Ben — I will miss Dr. Arkley and Turner (the principal's dog).

Austin — I like going to the Good News Chair because you always listen to my good news like when I got my twin nephews.

Michael — I like the Good News Chair to show you my writing.

Leland — I went to the Good News Chair when I finished my subtraction test. You were really proud of me!

Travis — I remember when Leland, Ben, and I were picking up trash on the playground and we got to go to the Good News Chair.

Austin — I like to go to the Good News Chair because you always write down what I say.

Rebecca — I remember the very first time that I was a car rider and I visited Dr. Arkley at the Good News Chair.

Lauren — I went to the Good News Chair when I lost my tooth.

Noah — I remember when I wrote my first book and I was so nervous to share it with you.

Dylan — I went to the Good News Chair when I put capitals and periods in my writer's notebook.

Ben — I will miss you when you leave because I like to go to the Good News Chair.

Beth — I like going to the Good News Chair because you like listening to me read.

Peter — I feel happy because you're always there when I go to the Good News Chair.

Stephanie — I like to go to the Good News Chair because when I read a story to Dr. Arkley and Turner I sometimes get a pencil.

Malik — I got to the Good News Chair for the first time when I was in pre-k and I lost my first tooth.

Cory — I will miss you.

THE PRINCIPAL'S DOG
AND A FRIEND

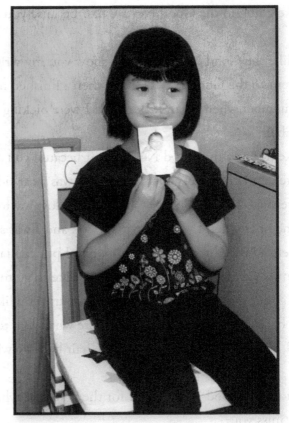

A NEW SISTER

WE HAVE GOOD NEWS

BUG BUDDIES

About Author

As a retired early childhood and elementary school principal and teacher, and as a parent and grandparent, Harriet Arkley, Ed.D., has spent a lifetime working with and caring for young children. This dedication started when she was a nineteen-year-old camp counselor living in a teepee on Lopez Island, part of the San Juan Islands of Washington. "I learned how important it is to keep my eye on what is right for each child and how to send them into the world feeling confident, worthy, special, and secure," says Arkley about her time with children.

She now co-coordinates a gardening program for young children and their parents in Bellingham, Washington, is a literacy volunteer at a neighborhood elementary school, and delights in every minute spent with her granddaughter. There is time too for hiking in the Cascades, spoiling her Golden Retriever, being entertained by their tuxedo cat, knitting, traveling, and spending lots of time with family and friends.

VISIT OUR WEBSITE
WWW.GOODNEWSCHAIR.COM

CPSIA information can be obtained at www.ICGtesting.com
Printed in the USA
LVOW02s2317260714

396190LV00013B/47/P